Survey of Credit Underwriting Practices

2010

Office of the Comptroller of the Currency
August 2010

Contents

Survey of Credit Underwriting Practices
2010

Introduction

The Office of the Comptroller of the Currency (OCC) conducted its 16th annual underwriting survey to identify trends in lending standards and credit risk for the most common types of commercial and retail credit offered by national banks. The survey covered the 12-month period ending March 31, 2010.

The 2010 survey included examiner assessments of credit underwriting standards at 51 of the largest national banks with assets of $3 billion or more. Examiners reported on loan products greater than 2 percent of the company's committed loan portfolio or more than $10 billion in committed exposure. The OCC recognizes that banks not meeting these thresholds may offer a full suite of products; because of the size of the product portfolios, examiners did not gather information on them for the purposes of this report. The survey covered loans totaling $4 trillion as of December 31, 2009, which represented approximately 93 percent of total loans in the national banking system at that time. Large banks discussed in this report are the 14 largest banks by asset size supervised by the OCC's Large Bank Supervision Department; the other 37 banks are supervised by the OCC's Midsize/Community Bank Supervision Department.

OCC examiners assigned to each bank assessed overall credit trends for 20 commercial and retail credit products. For the purposes of this survey, commercial credit included the following 13 categories:

- agricultural
- asset-based lending
- commercial construction
- residential construction
- other commercial real estate
- commercial leasing
- international
- large corporate
- leveraged
- middle market
- small business
- hedge funds – direct lending exposure
- hedge funds – counterparty credit exposure

Retail credit included the following seven categories:

- affordable housing
- credit cards
- indirect consumer paper
- conventional home equity
- high loan-to-value (HLTV) home equity
- other direct consumer
- residential first mortgages

"Underwriting standards," as used in this report, refers to the terms and conditions under which banks extend or renew credit, such as financial and collateral requirements, repayment programs, maturities, pricing, and covenants. Conclusions about "easing" or "tightening" represent OCC examiners' observations during the survey period. A conclusion that the underwriting standards for a particular loan category have eased or tightened does not necessarily indicate that all the standards for that particular category have been adjusted. Rather, the conclusion indicates that the adjustments that did occur had the net effect of easing or tightening the aggregate conditions under which banks extended credit.

Part I of this report summarizes the overall findings of the survey. Part II depicts the survey findings in data graphs. Part III presents the raw data used to develop the survey's principal findings and to create the data graphs. (Note: Some percentages in tables and figures do not add to 100 because of rounding.)

Part I: Overall Results

Primary Findings

- Overall, underwriting standards continued to tighten during the survey period (March 2009 – March 2010) for both commercial and retail loans, but at a lower rate than the 2009 survey. In certain products, the OCC is beginning to see some evidence of banks once again loosening standards in response to competition and a modest improvement in credit market liquidity.
- Loan portfolios that experienced the most tightening in underwriting during the 2010 survey period included credit card, home equity, residential and commercial construction, large corporate, and leveraged loans. It should be noted that, subsequent to the survey, our examiners have seen some evidence of problematic leveraged lending practices reemerging.
- As in the last two surveys, the health of the economy was a major factor influencing the tightening of credit standards. Examiners reported that the economic outlook was the most important credit issue confronting banks and the primary reason changes were made to underwriting standards. Examiners also reported changing risk appetite and product performance influenced changes to underwriting standards.

- The level of credit risk in both commercial and retail portfolios increased compared with the previous survey year and is anticipated to increase over the next 12 months. This increase was largely because of the combined effects of loans that were previously underwritten with more liberal standards coupled with continued economic weakness.

- This year's survey again indicated that the majority of banks generally apply the same underwriting standards to loans underwritten with the intent to hold as to those underwritten with the intent to distribute. A key lesson learned from the financial market disruption is the need for bankers to apply sound, consistent underwriting standards regardless of whether a loan is originated with the intent to hold or sell.

Commentary on Credit Risk

The financial market disruption of 2008 continued to affect bankers' appetite for risk and resulted in a renewed focus by bank lenders on fundamental credit principles. For the 12 months covered by the 2010 survey, examiners reported tightening of underwriting standards for commercial products in 65 percent of banks and for retail products in 74 percent of banks, compared with 86 percent and 83 percent in the 2009 survey. The tightening of standards reported in the last three surveys reflected continuing concerns about unfavorable external conditions and product performance. On a product-by-product basis, tightening was most significant for credit cards, home equity, construction lending, large corporate lending, and leveraged lending. International loans and counterparty risk to hedge funds showed net easing of underwriting standards.

For the second straight year, examiners reported that the surveyed banks used pricing as their primary method to modify underwriting standards for commercial products. Loan covenants and collateral requirements were also increasingly used to tighten standards. Covenants, as well as other structural underwriting criteria, afford banks a greater measure of control in managing credit risk. Examiners also noted fewer approved exceptions to policy.

Examiners reported continued tightening of retail underwriting standards across all products but at a slower rate than in 2009. The number of banks tightening standards declined slightly while the number of banks leaving retail underwriting standards unchanged increased. The principal reasons for tightening overall retail product underwriting standards included a changing economic outlook, portfolio quality and performance, and risk appetite. However, for credit cards, examiners also cited the Credit CARD Act of 2009 and its potential effects on portfolio performance as a reason banks tightened underwriting standards. Tightening was most often accomplished by changing the scorecard cutoff (e.g., requiring a higher minimum score for credit approval), followed by changes to pricing and enhanced documentation, collateral, and debt-service requirements.

Examiners reported selective easing for 3 percent of retail products offered. For the few banks easing standards on select products, examiners cited the banks' improving economic outlook and increased risk appetite as the primary reasons for relaxing underwriting standards.

Despite tightening standards, examiners reported that the overall level of credit risk increased in retail and commercial portfolios during the survey period, and they expect the level of risk to continue to increase over the next 12 months. At the time of the survey, examiners expected credit risk to increase in all products offered but more recently, the OCC has observed that risk may have stabilized in certain products. Increased risk was primarily attributed to increasing levels of problem loans because of the economy, escalating job losses, and decreased real estate values. Examiners indicated concerns with current levels of risk in essentially all product lines, with the most concern for residential and commercial construction, leveraged loans, and small business.

As noted earlier, examiners observed signs that some banks are loosening underwriting standards in response to competitive pressures. The OCC continues to remind bankers that underwriting standards should not be compromised by competitive pressures or the assumption that loans will be sold to third parties. In addition, bankers should continue to improve risk management practices through techniques such as portfolio stress testing and sensitivity analysis.

Commercial Underwriting Standards

For the third consecutive year, examiners reported a tightening in commercial credit standards for the 12 months ending March 31, 2010. As shown in table 1, the 2010 survey results indicated that 65 percent of the surveyed banks tightened commercial underwriting standards. Only 2 percent noted easing, with the remaining banks indicating that there was no change in the underwriting standards.

Table 1: Commercial Products						
	2005	2006	2007	2008	2009	2010
Eased	34%	31%	26%	6%	0%	2%
Unchanged	54%	63%	58%	42%	14%	33%
Tightened	12%	6%	16%	52%	86%	65%

Note: For additional information, see figure 1 on page 13.

Examiners cited the economic outlook, risk appetite, and product performance as the primary reasons for tightened standards across all product lines. While the economic outlook was a concern for all commercial products, it continued to be the most pronounced for commercial real estate (CRE) products. The disruption in financial markets remained an issue. The lack of liquidity in secondary markets and high refinancing risk continued to adversely affect leveraged finance, syndicated loan markets, and CRE products.

Credit spreads, or the compensation for assuming credit risk, continued to be the primary underwriting method that banks use to manage the credit risk in their loan portfolios. However, banks have also increased the use of covenants, collateral, guarantor support, and size of credit lines to control risks in their portfolios. As the economy recovers and competition increases, the OCC expects banks to maintain prudent underwriting standards.

Selected Product Trends

Underwriting standards tightened for all commercial loan products surveyed. The most prevalent tightening occurred in CRE loans, leveraged loans, and small business loans. Examiners reported a net increase in credit risk for all commercial credit products, with the exception of hedge funds, where exposures were dramatically reduced.

Commercial Real Estate

CRE products include residential construction, commercial construction, and other CRE loans. Almost all of the surveyed banks offered these CRE products. CRE remained a primary concern among examiners, given the past rapid growth of these exposures and banks' significant concentrations relative to their capital. Net tightening, which measures the difference between the percentage of banks tightening and the percentage of those easing, was greatest in commercial construction, followed by residential construction and other commercial real estate.

Examiners most often cited the distressed real estate market and poor product performance as the reason for net tightening. Examiners indicated that overall CRE credit risk increased at 92 percent of the banks since the previous survey and is expected to increase during the next survey year at 85 percent of the banks. Driving the assessment of increased credit risk were external conditions, downward trends in collateral values, weakening debt service capacity, and current and expected levels of problem loans.

The next three tables provide the breakdown by each real estate type.

Twenty-two banks (or 43 percent) of the 51 banks in the survey offered residential construction loan products. This product's performance has been poor due to weak economic conditions resulting in high levels of problem loans and losses. Table 2 shows that 64 percent of banks surveyed for the 2010 survey tightened underwriting standards for residential construction while none reported easing standards.

Table 2: Residential Construction						
	2005	**2006**	**2007**	**2008**	**2009**	**2010**
Eased	21%	25%	17%	2%	0%	0%
Unchanged	72%	64%	50%	36%	8%	36%
Tightened	7%	11%	33%	62%	92%	64%

Note: For additional information, see tables on page 32.

Thirty-six or (or 70 percent) of the banks offered commercial construction loans. Examiners reported that the continued economic downturn, job losses, and weak consumer spending adversely affected the retail, office, apartment, and industrial sectors. Examiners were most concerned about retail properties because of low consumer confidence and spending levels, weak retail sales, increased store closings, and increased numbers of bankruptcy and liquidations in the retail sector.

Table 3 shows that 72 percent of banks surveyed for this report tightened underwriting standards for commercial construction while only 3 percent reported easing standards.

Table 3: Commercial Construction						
	2005	**2006**	**2007**	**2008**	**2009**	**2010**
Eased	29%	32%	28%	8%	0%	3%
Unchanged	63%	56%	59%	43%	20%	25%
Tightened	8%	12%	13%	49%	80%	72%

Note: For additional information, see tables on page 31.

Nearly all banks offered a variety of CRE loans for purposes other than residential or commercial construction. For purposes of this survey the OCC broadly grouped these loans together under the "Other CRE" category. As with commercial residential and commercial construction, examiners reported that this sector's declining underlying values, increasing vacancy rates, and significant reduction in permanent market liquidity triggered a change in risk appetite. In some cases, failed syndications resulted in banks retaining a higher level of originated loans on their balance sheets than anticipated. Table 4 shows that 60 percent of banks surveyed tightened underwriting standards for other CRE while 2 percent reported easing standards.

Table 4: Other CRE						
	2005	**2006**	**2007**	**2008**	**2009**	**2010**
Eased	24%	32%	20%	2%	2%	2%
Unchanged	65%	60%	73%	73%	22%	38%
Tightened	11%	8%	7%	25%	76%	60%

Note: For additional information, see tables on page 33.

Small Business Loans

Examiners reported that 32 of the 51 surveyed banks offered small business loans. The OCC noted definitions of small business lending varied among the surveyed banks. However, regardless of varying definitions, examiners reported tightened underwriting standards and increased risk for small business in line with other surveyed products. Examiners cited changes in the company's financial condition, combined with the economic outlook, as the major reasons for tightened credit.

Examiners indicated that small business credit risk increased in 85 percent of the banks since the prior survey and expect the risk will continue to increase over the next year in 75 percent of the banks. Examiners most frequently cited changes in external conditions and portfolio quality as support for the increased level of risk. Table 5 shows that 66 percent of banks surveyed tightened underwriting standards for small business loans while none reported easing standards.

Table 5: Small Business Loans						
	2005	**2006**	**2007**	**2008**	**2009**	**2010**
Eased	13%	19%	11%	11%	0%	0%
Unchanged	81%	76%	76%	72%	36%	34%
Tightened	6%	5%	13%	17%	64%	66%

Note: For additional information, see tables on page 36.

Leveraged Loans

While only 16 (or 31 percent) of the banks offered this product, the size of the portfolio was significant. Declining portfolio quality and changes in banks' risk appetite contributed to tightening standards. Banks primarily used credit spreads and maximum allowable leverage to tighten standards. Additionally, many banks are only working with existing borrowers and are not seeking to expand this portfolio.

Examiners reported that credit risk in this product increased at 88 percent of the banks since last year's survey and expect this risk to increase at 75 percent of the banks over the next year. Examiners stated that credit risk in this product will likely increase as economic challenges affect refinancing risk and market liquidity. Because of the challenges facing these borrowers, examiners expect that the levels of criticized and classified credits in these portfolios are likely to increase through 2010. Table 6 shows that 75 percent of banks surveyed tightened underwriting standards for leveraged loans while none reported easing standards.

Table 6: Leveraged Loans						
	2005	**2006**	**2007**	**2008**	**2009**	**2010**
Eased	32%	61%	67%	20%	0%	0%
Unchanged	68%	31%	33%	20%	31%	25%
Tightened	0%	8%	0%	60%	69%	75%

Note: For additional information, see tables on page 37.

Originate to Hold Versus Originate to Sell

This is the third annual survey to assess the differences in underwriting between loans originated to hold in the banks' own loan portfolios and loans originated to sell in the marketplace. The OCC expects national banks to underwrite loans based on sound underwriting standards regardless of their intent to hold or sell the loan, and to apply the same general standards for both types of lending.

As shown in table 7, there has been significant improvement in this area. Of the 51 banks surveyed, 23 percent originated loans both to hold and to sell. In this year's survey, examiners noted only 12 percent of banks offering leveraged loans and 10 percent offering international loans had different standards for loans originated to hold than for loans originated to sell, compared with 67 percent and 40 percent in 2008. The continued tightening of underwriting standards for all loans, whether intended for sale or investment, was a direct result of changes in the economic outlook and market liquidity. Recent activity has shown some signs of market resurgence with institutional investors returning to the primary market.

Table 7: Hold Versus Sell Underwriting Standards			
Product	**Underwritten Differently**		
	2008	**2009**	**2010**
Leveraged Loans	67%	38%	12%
International	40%	0%	10%
Large Corporate	21%	21%	3%
Asset-Based Loans	33%	13%	0%
CRE – Commercial Residential Construction	17%	17%	0%
CRE – Commercial Construction	20%	10%	0%
CRE – Other	20%	9%	0%

Retail Underwriting Standards

As noted in table 8, examiners reported continued tightening of retail underwriting standards in the 2010 survey, although the number of banks tightening declined slightly. Lending standards were tightened in 74 percent of reporting banks, down from 83 percent in 2009. The number of banks leaving retail underwriting standards unchanged increased. Of the 70 percent of the surveyed banks that tightened underwriting standards during the survey period, examiners reported the banks as having conservative underwriting standards. Underwriting standards were reported as moderate for another 26 percent of the banks which tightened their standards. Only one bank that tightened its standards had underwriting standards considered to be somewhat liberal.

Table 8: Overall Retail Products by Banks						
	2005	**2006**	**2007**	**2008**	**2009**	**2010**
Eased	28%	28%	20%	0%	0%	0%
Unchanged	62%	65%	67%	32%	17%	26%
Tightened	10%	7%	13%	68%	83%	74%

Note: For additional information, see figure 9 on page 21.

Conservative underwriting standards were most prevalent in community banks where 83 percent of the surveyed banks' standards were considered conservative. The percentage of midsize and large banks with conservative underwriting standards was 68 percent and 62 percent, respectively. However, tightening most often occurred in large banks (84 percent) followed by community and midsize banks at 72 percent and 68 percent, respectively.

Survey responses reflected tightened standards for 58 percent of individual retail products compared with 71 percent in 2009. Underwriting standards remained unchanged for 39 percent of retail product offerings, up from 29 percent in the 2009 survey. The principal reasons for tightening specific retail product underwriting standards included a changing economic outlook, portfolio quality and performance, and changing risk appetites. For credit card lenders, the Credit CARD Act and its potential effects on portfolio performance and profitability were also cited as a reason why banks tightened underwriting standards. Tightening was most often accomplished by changing the scorecard cutoff (e.g, requiring a higher minimum score for credit approval), followed by changes to pricing and enhanced documentation, collateral, and debt-service requirements.

Only five of the product-specific surveys indicated an easing of underwriting standards. Examiners cited the banks' views that the economic outlook for these products had improved along with the banks' increased risk appetite as the primary reasons for relaxing standards. Two of the five responses indicated "change in regulatory policies/guidelines" as a reason for easing. In these cases, underwriting standards were eased either to conform to the government-sponsored enterprise requirements or to conform to the requirements of a government-guaranteed lending program. Despite the easing noted in specific product standards, examiners reported the underwriting standards for these products overall as somewhat conservative. In only one bank were standards rated somewhat liberal. Overall retail credit underwriting standards for these banks had tightened or remained unchanged since the last survey.

Examiners reported increasing credit risk in all retail products covered by the survey. Increased risk was most pronounced in credit cards, home equity, residential real estate, and direct consumer lending. Concerns about the effects of general economic conditions and portfolio performance resulting from prior years' liberal underwriting remained the primary reasons for increased risk levels. Examiners expect retail credit risk to continue to increase in all retail products over the next year. The greatest increases in credit risk are expected to occur in high loan-to-value home equity loans, residential real estate, and conventional home equity products.

Examiners reported that 58 percent of banks exhibited good adherence to underwriting standards with exceptions well supported, while an additional 40 percent demonstrated acceptable adherence to underwriting standards. Approved exception trends indicated that 36 percent of respondents were decreasing the volume of approved exceptions while 53 percent experienced no change in volume. Approved exception volumes increased in only 7 percent of surveyed banks. Survey results indicated that 93 percent of respondents were tracking exceptions. Instances where exception tracking was lacking are isolated in individual products.

Selected Product Trends

The following sections discuss changes within various product groups.

Residential Real Estate

Examiners reported on residential real estate loans in 42 of the surveyed banks. As shown in tables 9, 10, and 11, tighter underwriting standards remained prevalent, although fewer banks incrementally tightened and more banks left underwriting standards unchanged. Underwriting standards remained conservative because of poor portfolio performance resulting from more liberal underwriting standards in prior years, particularly 2005 through 2007 originations, and continuing economic weakness.

Some banks responded to the ongoing residential real estate downturn by exiting certain lines of business. Three banks no longer offer affordable housing loans, four banks discontinued high loan-to-value home equity lending, and two banks stopped offering residential real estate loans during the survey period. Conversely, two banks eased underwriting standards for residential real estate and conventional home equity loans. Eased underwriting standards involved collateral requirements, document requirements, pricing, scorecard cutoff, and amortization requirements. Despite this easing, these institutions maintained conservative underwriting standards for these products.

Table 9: Residential Real Estate						
	2005	**2006**	**2007**	**2008**	**2009**	**2010**
Eased	22%	26%	19%	0%	0%	5%
Unchanged	73%	69%	67%	44%	27%	36%
Tightened	5%	5%	14%	56%	73%	59%

Note: For additional information, see tables on page 47.

Table 10: Home Equity – Conventional						
	2005	**2006**	**2007**	**2008**	**2009**	**2010**
Eased	27%	34%	19%	2%	0%	5%
Unchanged	62%	64%	65%	46%	22%	35%
Tightened	11%	2%	16%	52%	78%	60%

Note: For additional information, see tables on page 44.

Table 11: Home Equity – High LTV						
	2005	**2006**	**2007**	**2008**	**2009**	**2010**
Eased	24%	37%	22%	6%	0%	0%
Unchanged	56%	63%	61%	6%	7%	13%
Tightened	20%	0%	17%	89%	93%	87%

Note: For additional information, see tables on page 45.

Credit Cards

Banks continued to tighten credit card underwriting standards in 2009 in response to weak economic conditions, high unemployment, heavy consumer debt loads, and portfolio performance. In addition, examiners cited the new Credit CARD Act and its potential effects on portfolio performance and profitability as another reason banks tightened credit card underwriting standards. Of the banks that tightened standards, the Credit CARD Act was cited as a reason in 62 percent of the banks.

As shown in table 12, 81 percent of surveyed institutions tightened underwriting standards compared with 68 percent last year. No banks eased credit card standards. Examiners reported that credit risk increased in 94 percent of banks compared with 90 percent in the 2009 survey. Credit risk is expected to increase in 62 percent of banks in 2010 as consumers continue to be affected by the weak economy. However, the rate of increase is declining as more conservative lending standards become embedded in new originations and lenders work through existing portfolio problems.

The principal methods of tightening credit card underwriting standards were raising scorecard cutoffs, reducing maximum line size, increasing pricing and loan fees, tighter debt service requirements, and increasing minimum payment requirements.

Table 12: Credit Cards						
	2005	**2006**	**2007**	**2008**	**2009**	**2010**
Eased	7%	19%	16%	18%	0%	0%
Unchanged	74%	56%	79%	47%	32%	19%
Tightened	19%	25%	5%	35%	68%	81%

Note: For additional information, see tables on page 42.

Consumer Lending (Direct and Indirect)

In this survey, examiners reported on indirect consumer lending in 21 banks and direct consumer lending in 19 banks. Sixty percent of indirect lenders and one-third of direct lenders tightened underwriting standards in the past year. The remaining banks left underwriting standards unchanged except for one bank which eased indirect underwriting standards. Like real estate lending, examiners stated that underwriting standards tightened mainly due to continuing economic weakness and poor portfolio performance caused by the liberal underwriting standards of prior years.

Most significant was the number of banks exiting the consumer lending business. Four of the 21 banks reporting on indirect lending exited the line of business within the past 12 months and another one plans to do so in the coming year. In addition, five of the surveyed banks involved in direct consumer lending have exited this business within the past year or plan to do so during the coming year.

Originate to Hold Versus Originate to Sell

Ninety-eight percent of respondents originated retail loans to hold while 32 percent also originated loans for sale. Residential real estate loans were originated for sale by 78 percent of the surveyed banks and affordable housing loans were originated for sale by 32 percent. Approximately 20 percent of surveyed banks utilized different underwriting standards for products originated for sale. One-third of the surveyed banks changed underwriting standards for residential real estate loans originated for sale. Loan pricing, scorecard cutoffs, debt service requirements, and collateral requirements were the underwriting criteria that most often distinguished loans held in portfolio from those originated for sale.

Part II: Data Graphs

Note: Some percentages used to create the data graphs do not add to 100 because of rounding.

Figure 1: Overall Credit Underwriting Trends – Commercial

(Percent of Responses)

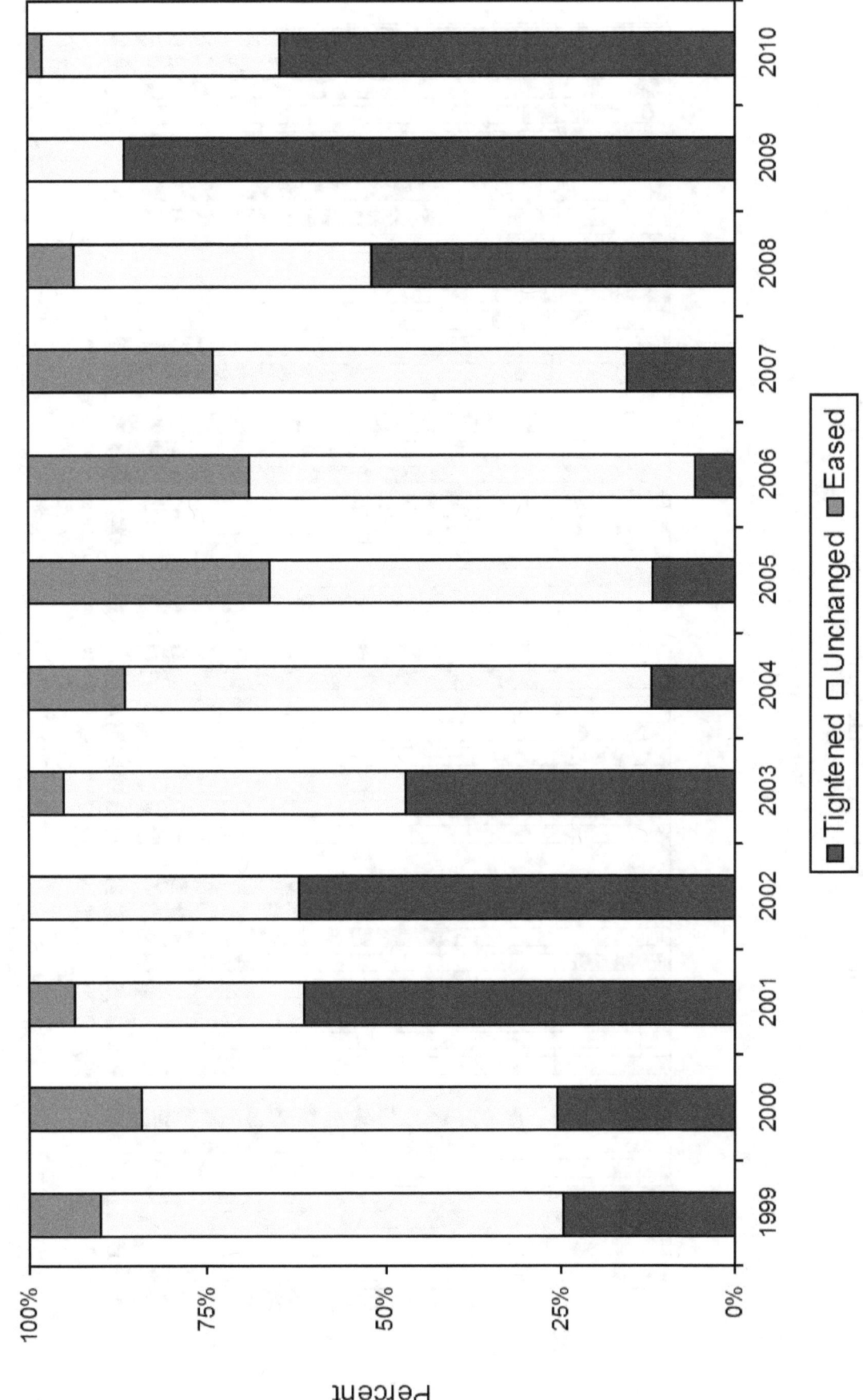

■ Tightened □ Unchanged ■ Eased

Figure 2: Commercial Underwriting Trends, by Product Type

(Percent of Responses)

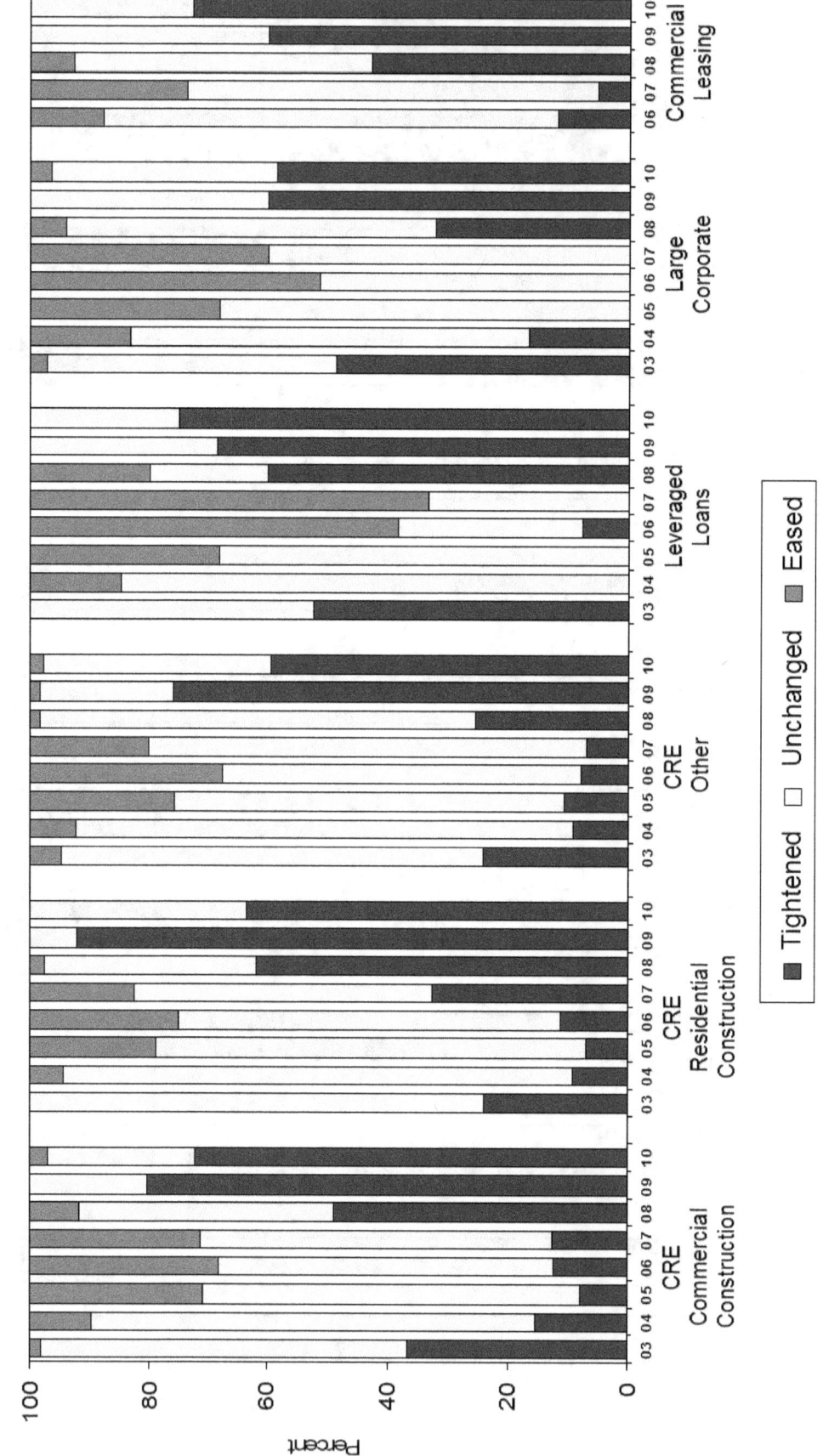

Figure 3: Commercial Underwriting Trends, by Product Type (Continued)

(Percent of Responses)

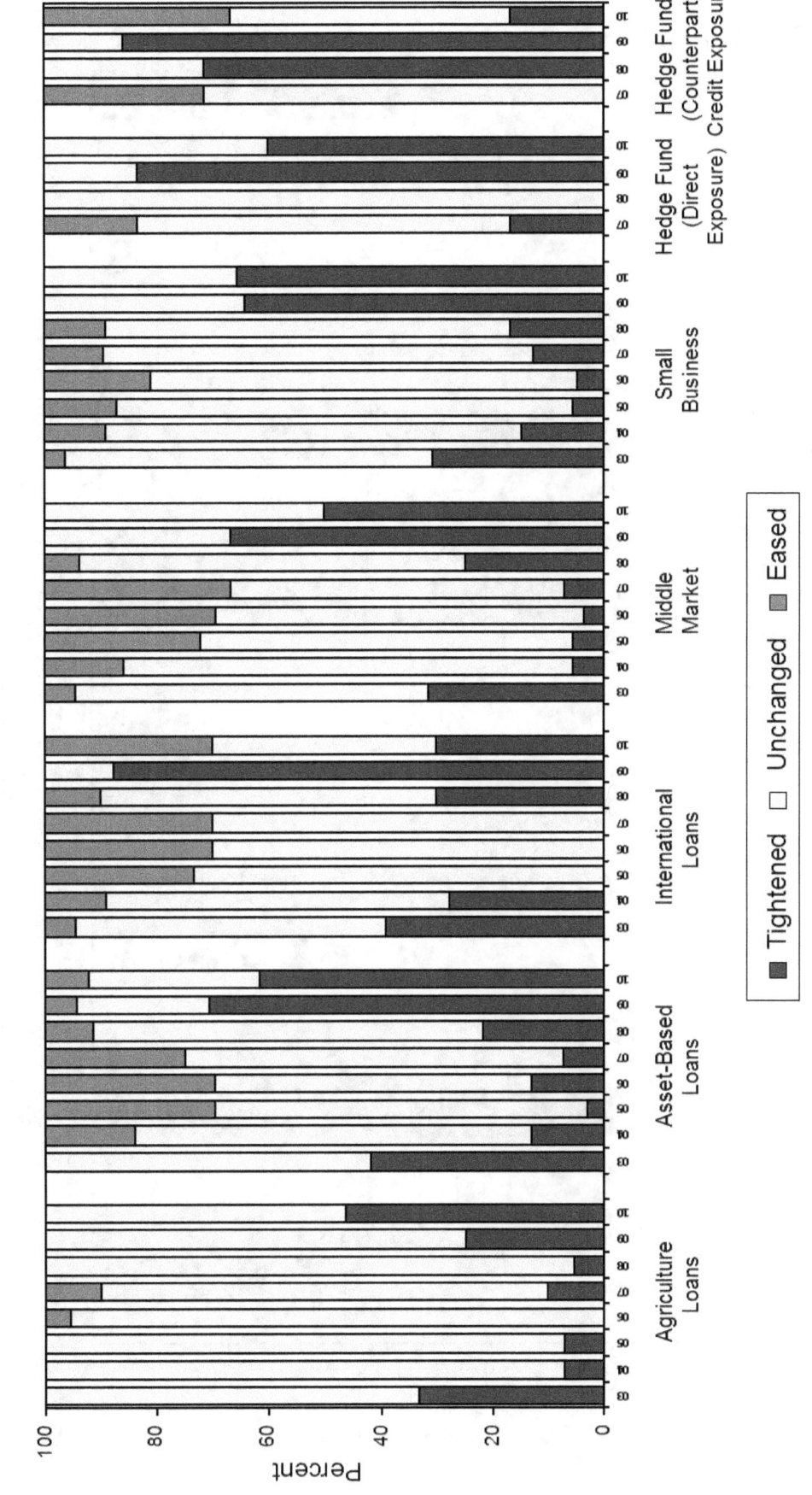

Figure 4: Reasons for Changing Commercial Underwriting Standards

(Percent of Responses)

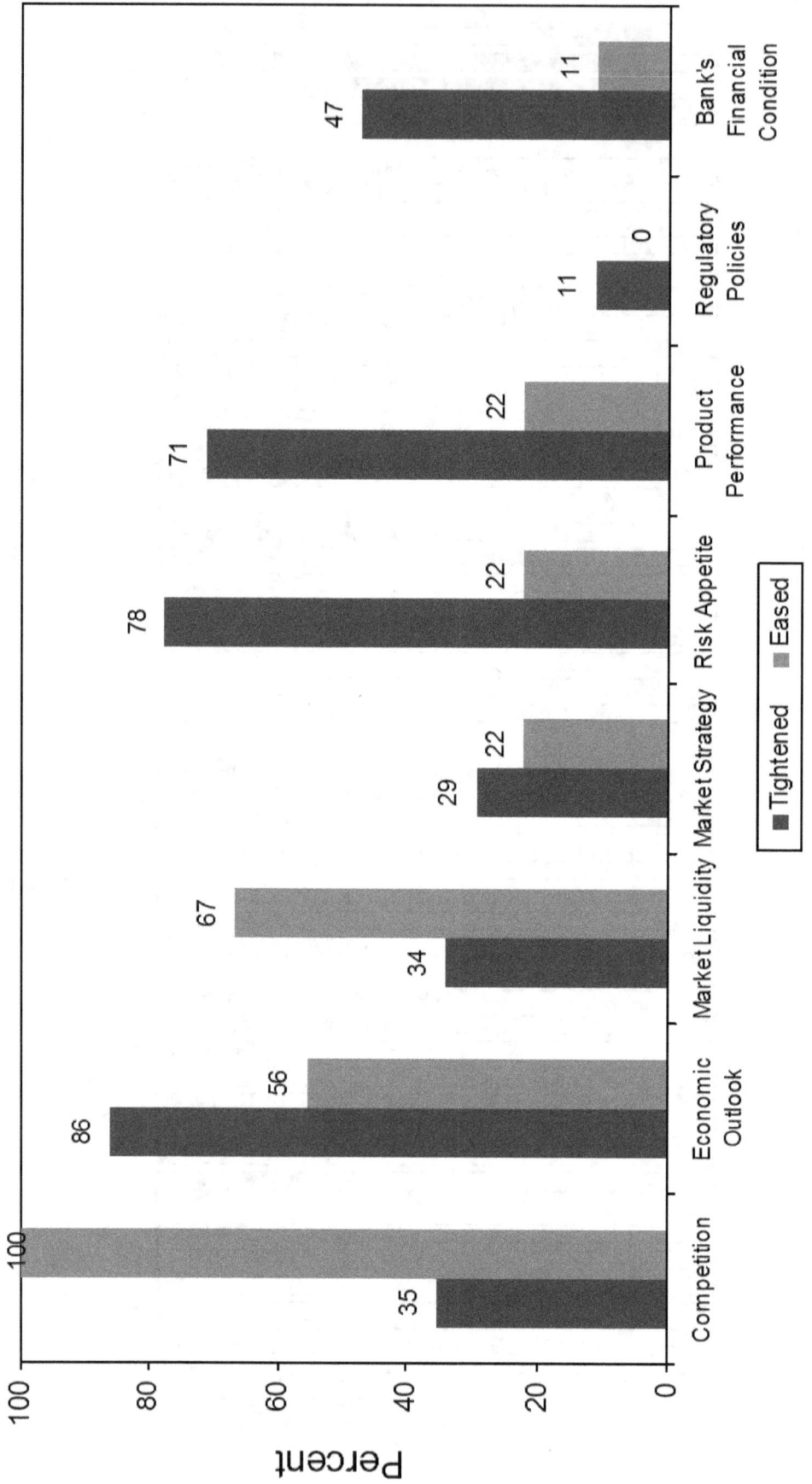

Figure 5: Methods Used to Change Commercial Underwriting Standards

(Percent of Responses)

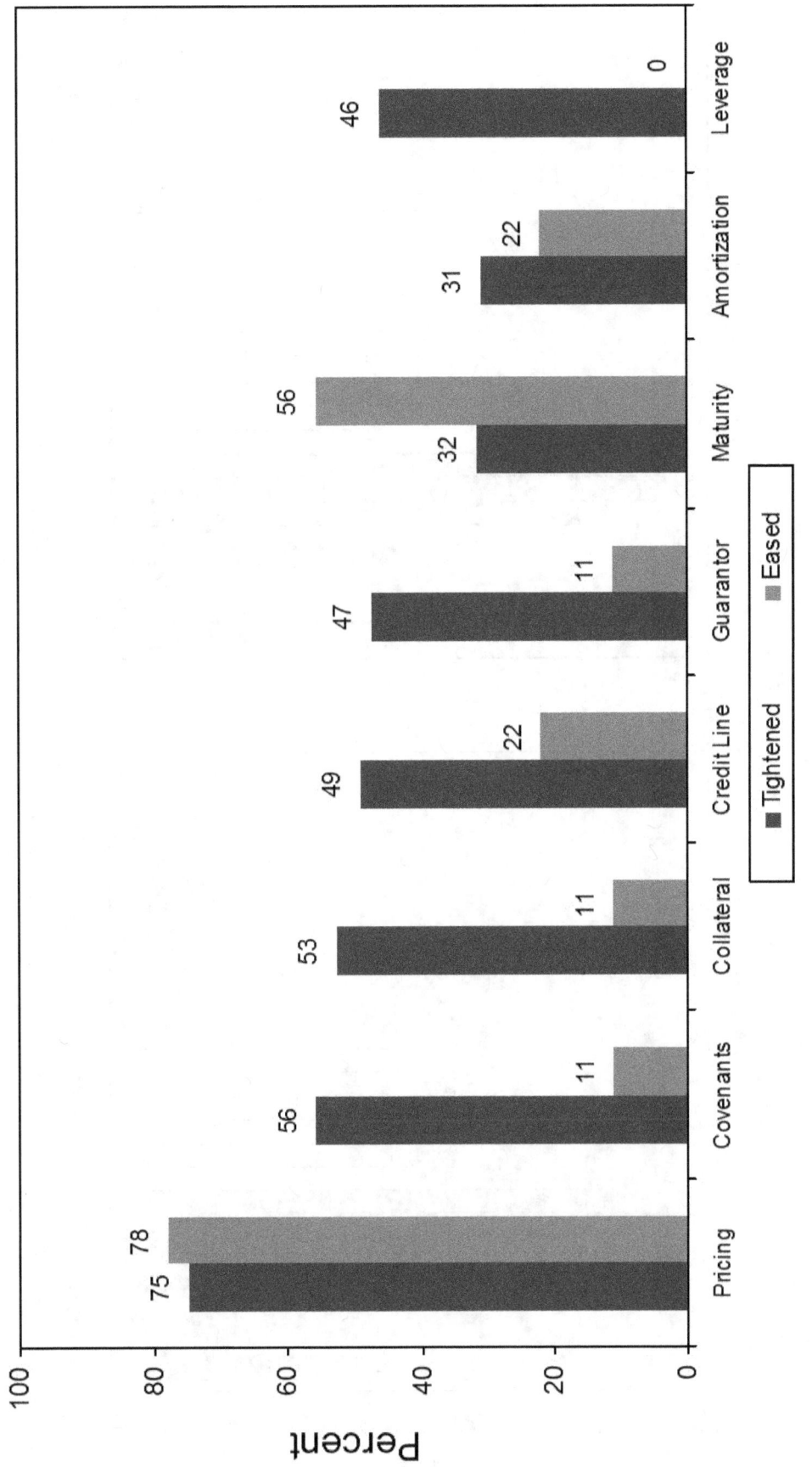

Figure 6: Commercial Credit Risk – Direction of Change and Outlook

(Percent of Responses)

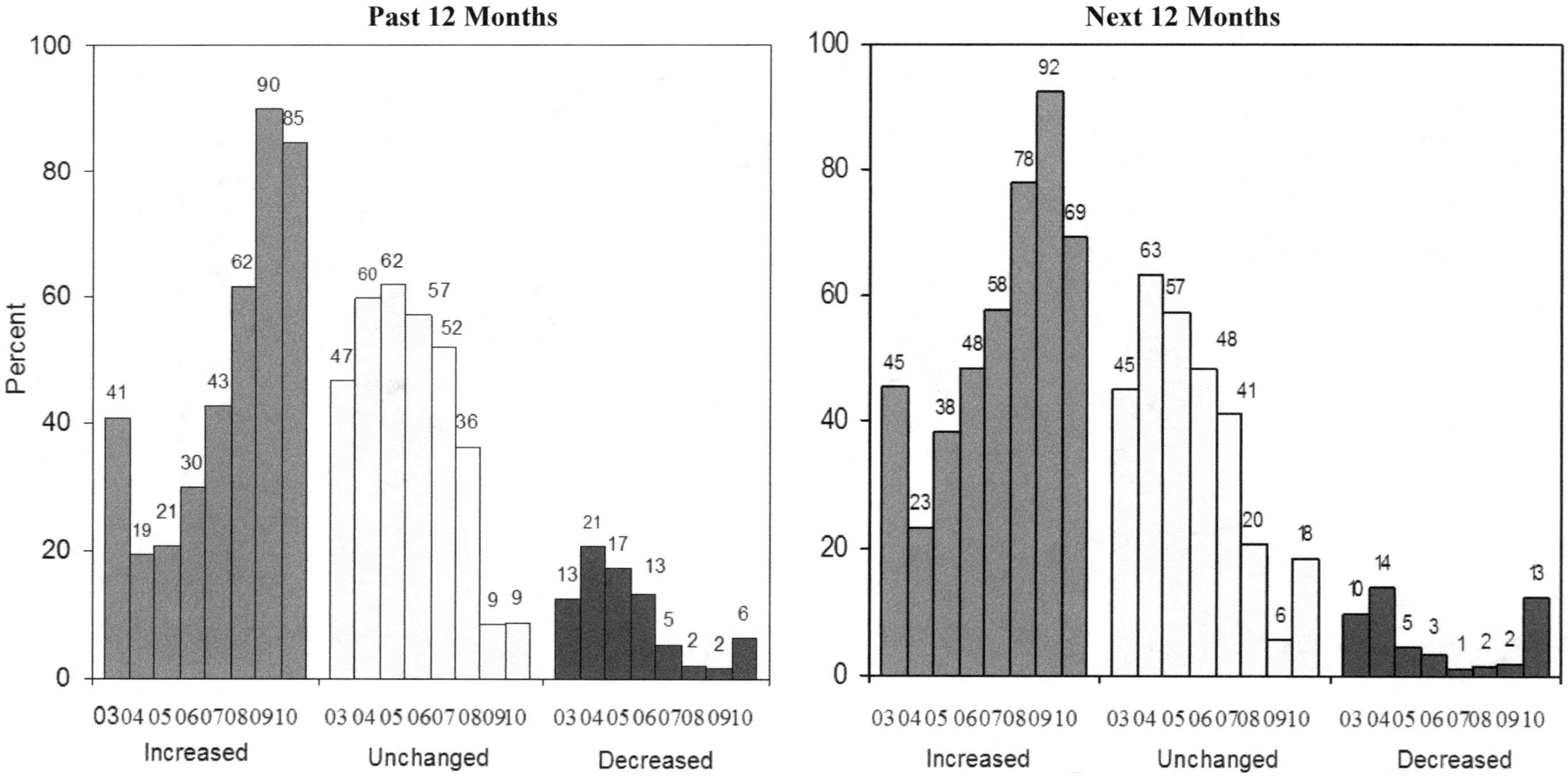

Figure 7: Commercial Credit Risk Trends – Current Credit Risk Change, by Product Type

(Percent of Responses)

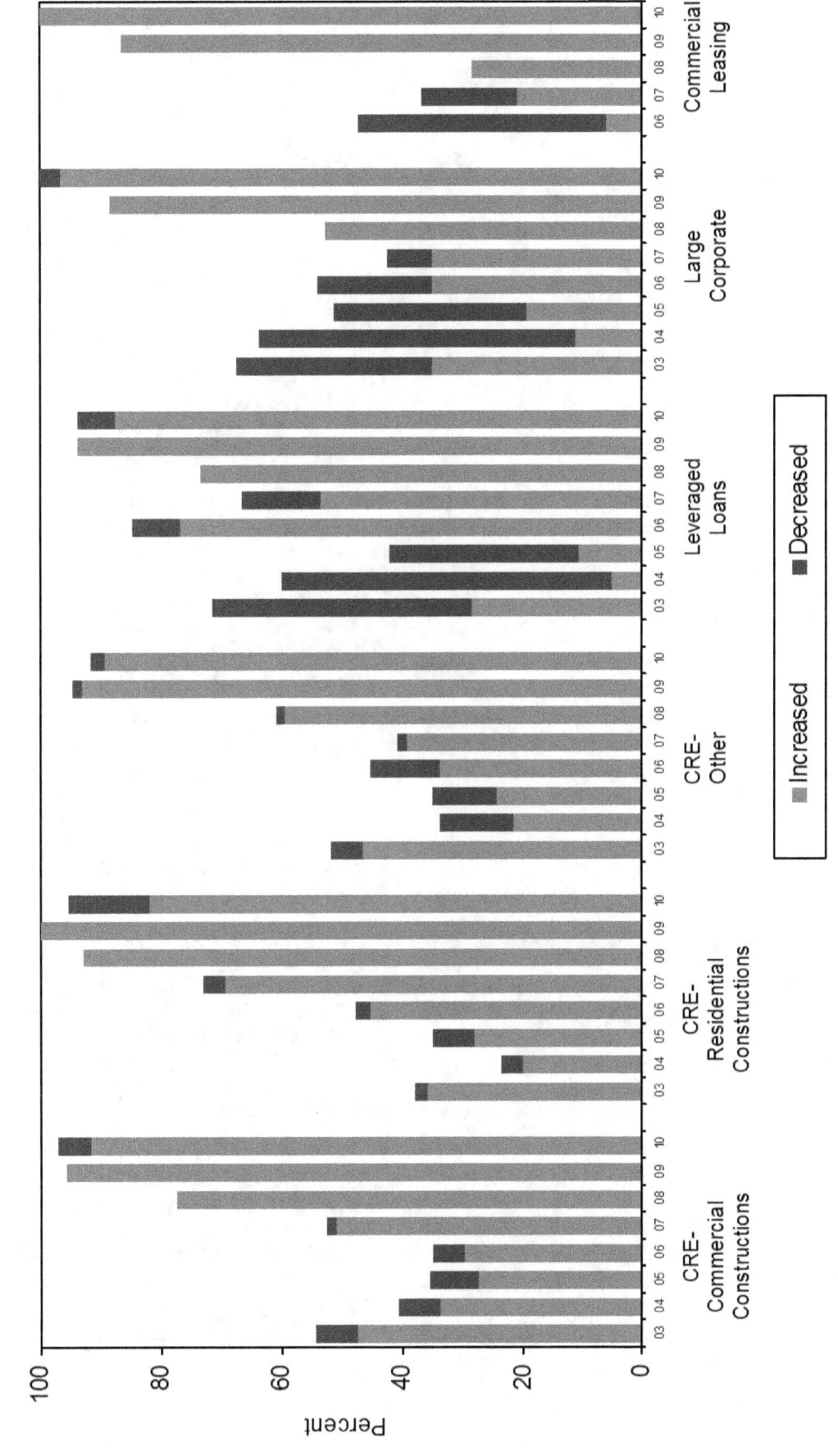

Figure 8: Commercial Credit Risk Trends – Current Credit Risk Change, by Product Type (Continued)

(Percent of Responses)

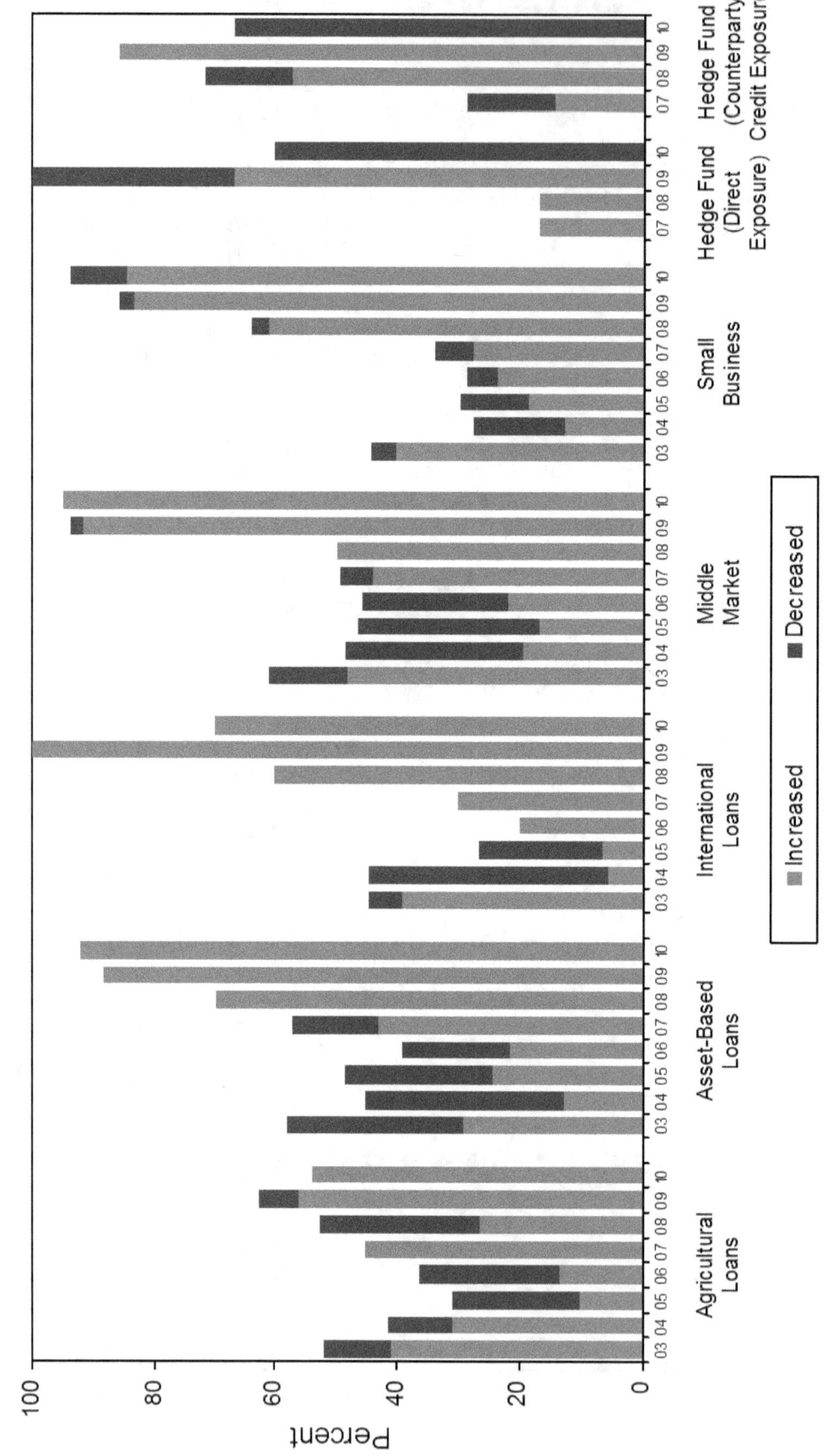

Figure 9: Overall Credit Underwriting Trends – Retail

(Percent of Responses)

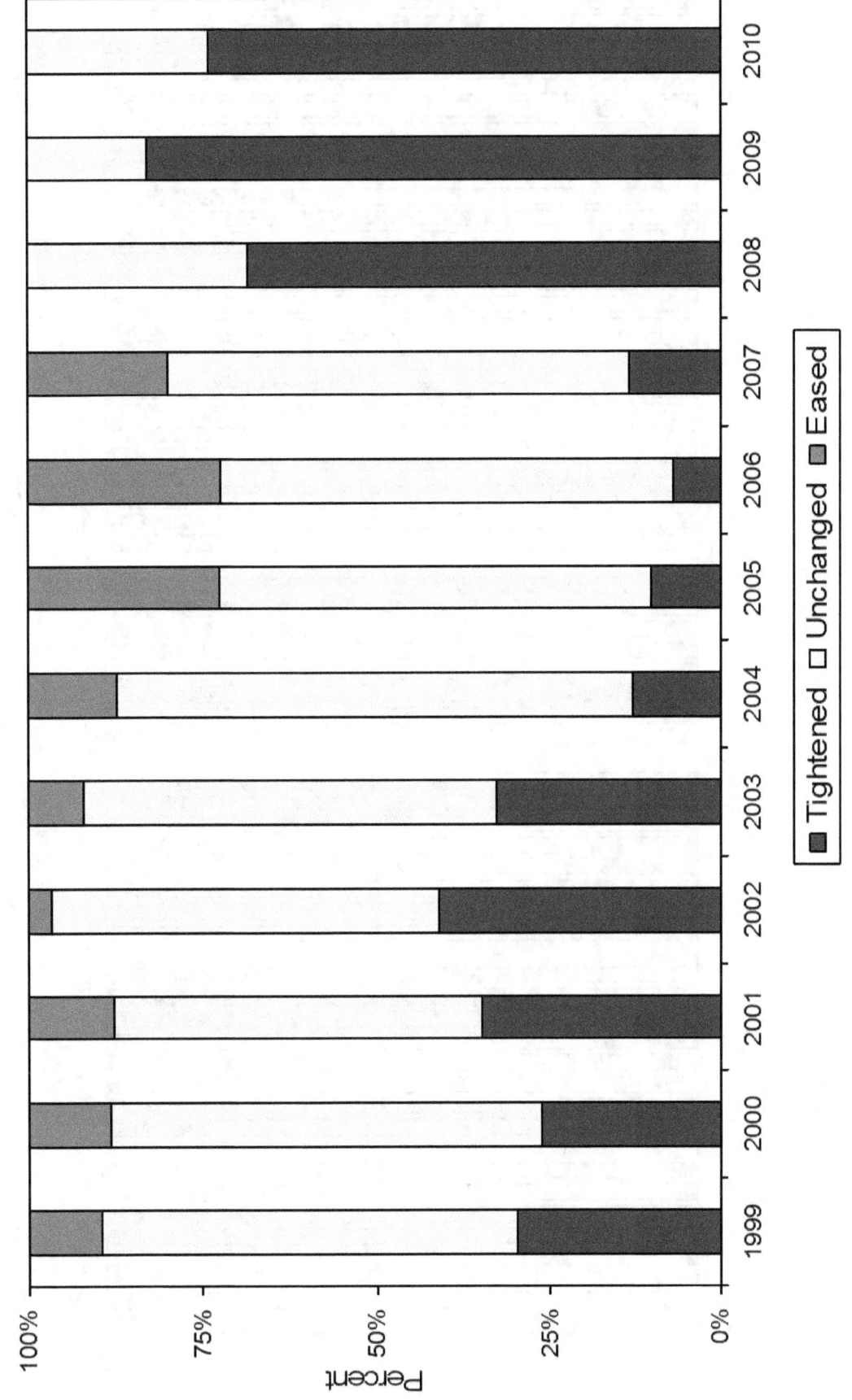

Figure 10: Retail Underwriting Trends, by Product Type

(Percent of Responses)

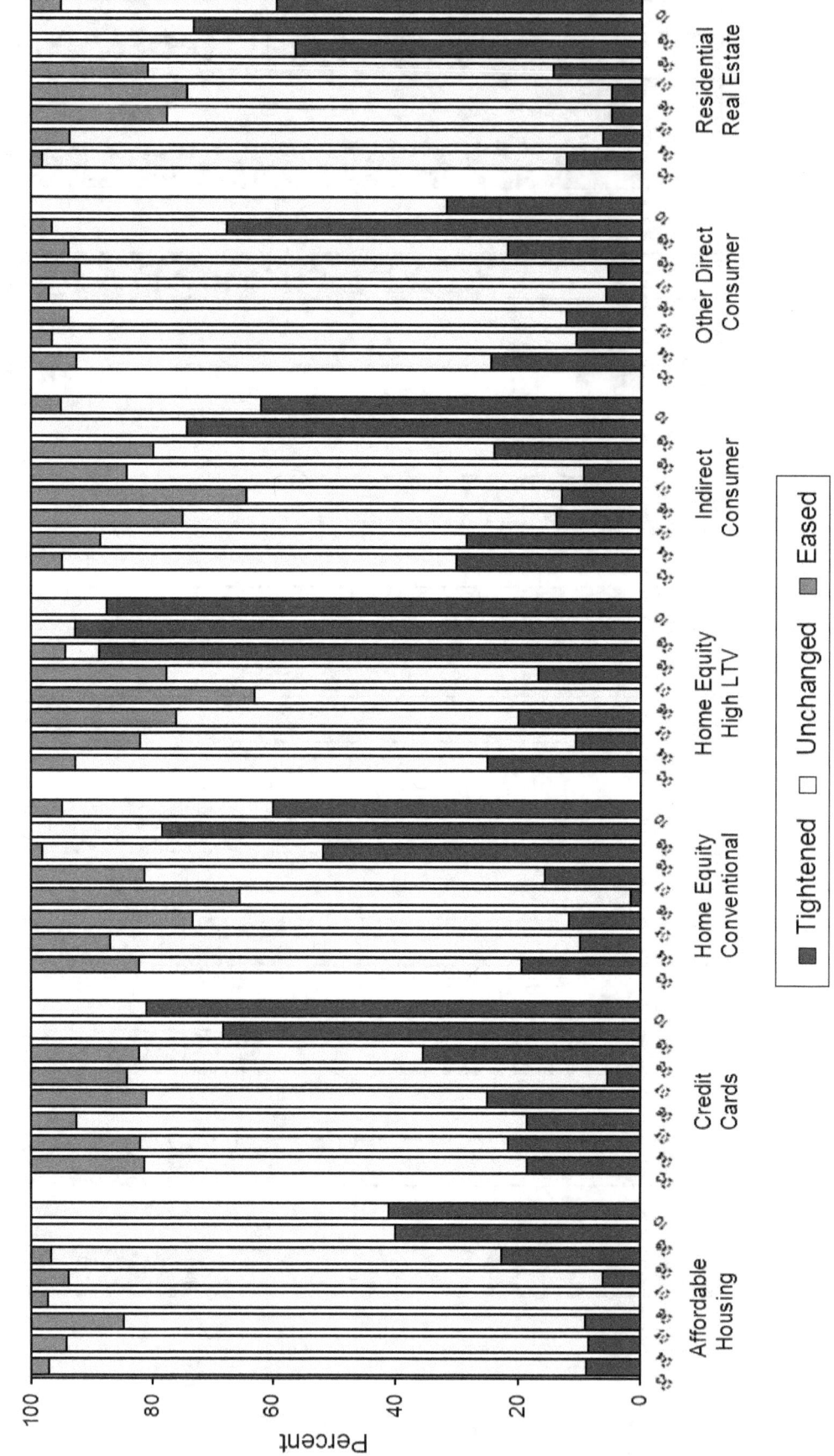

Figure 11: Reasons for Changing Retail Underwriting Standards

(Percent of Responses)

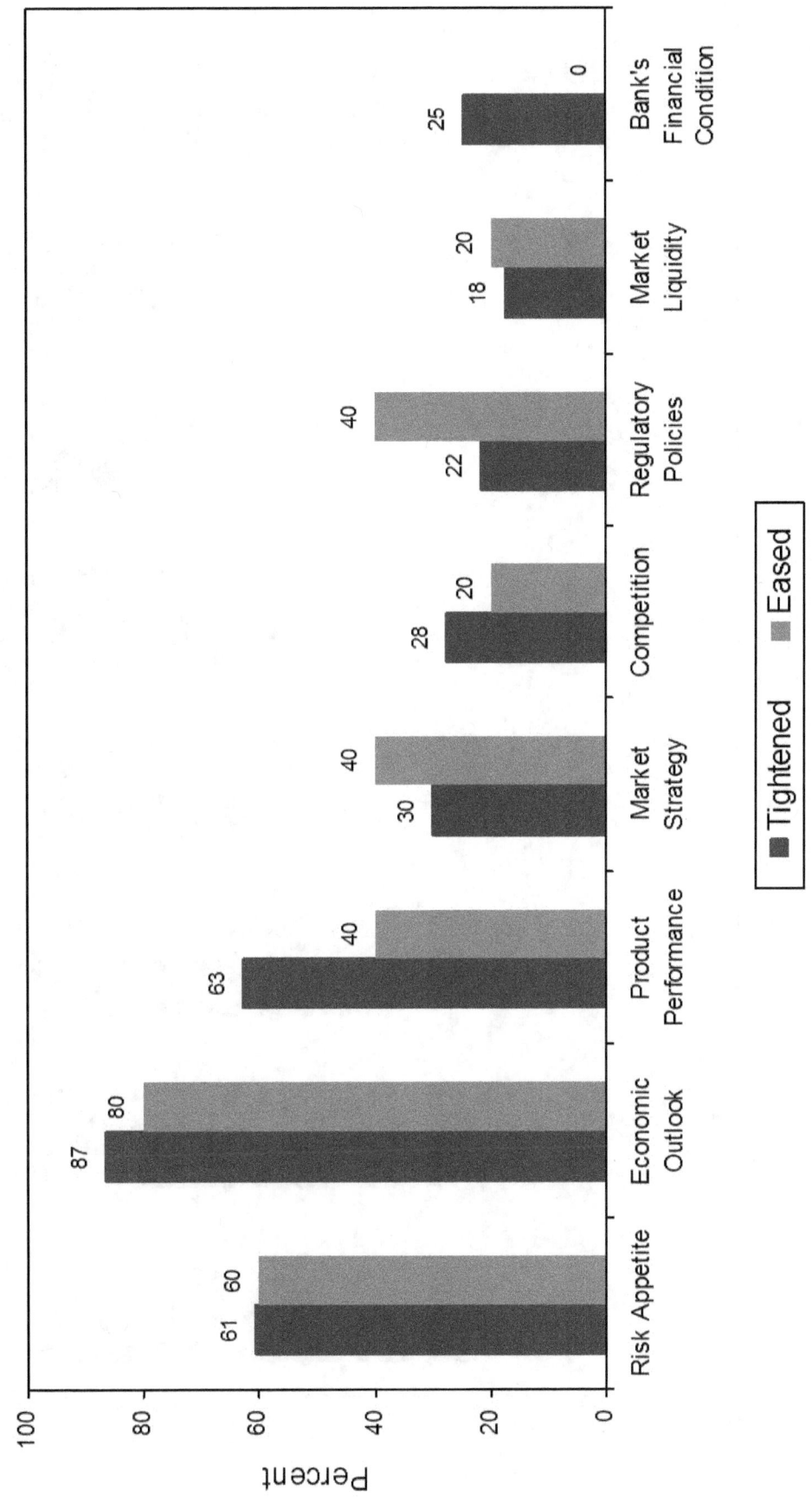

Figure 12: Methods Used to Change Retail Underwriting Standards

(Percent of Responses)

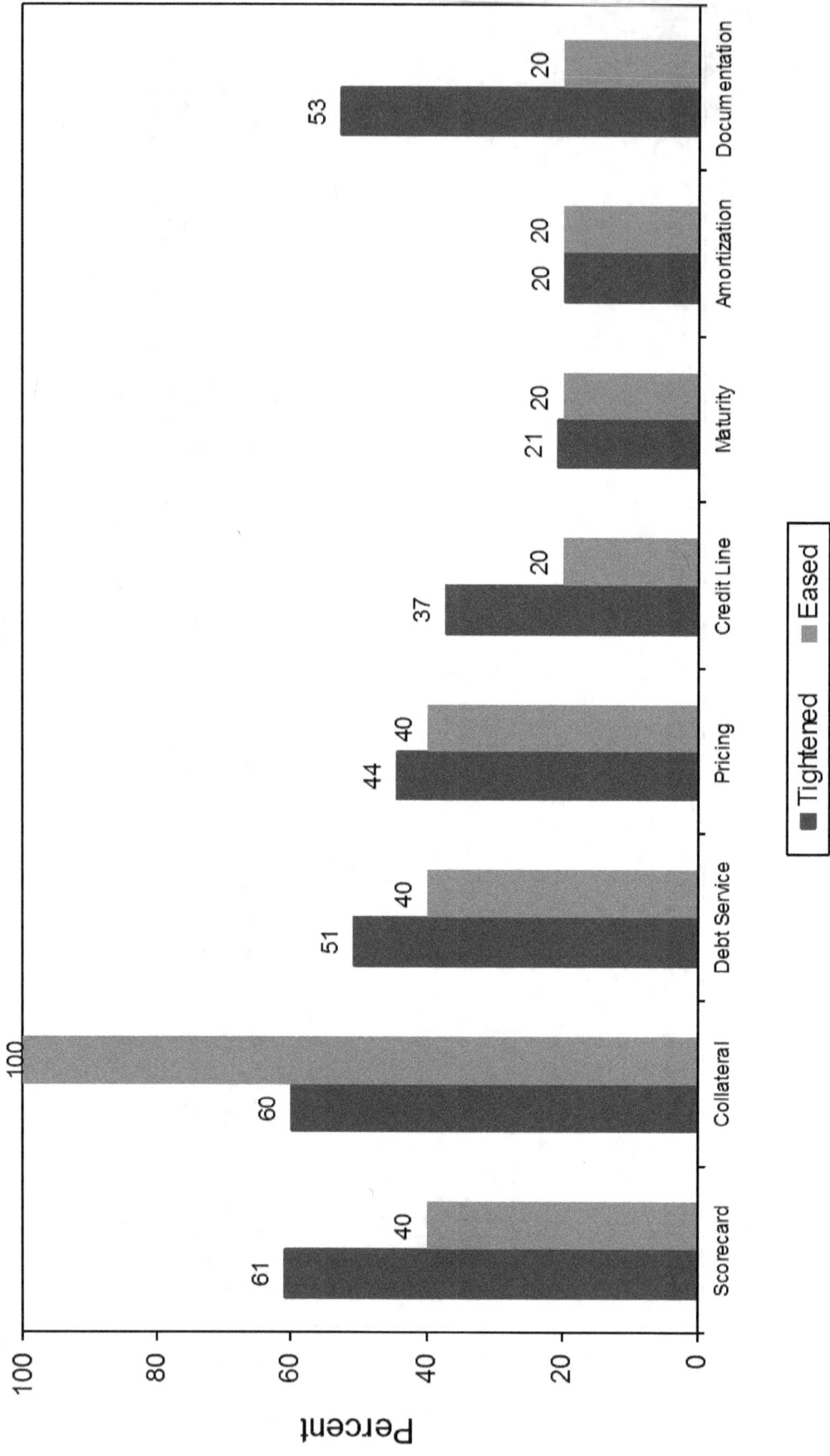

Figure 13: Retail Credit Risk – Direction of Change and Outlook

(Percent of Responses)

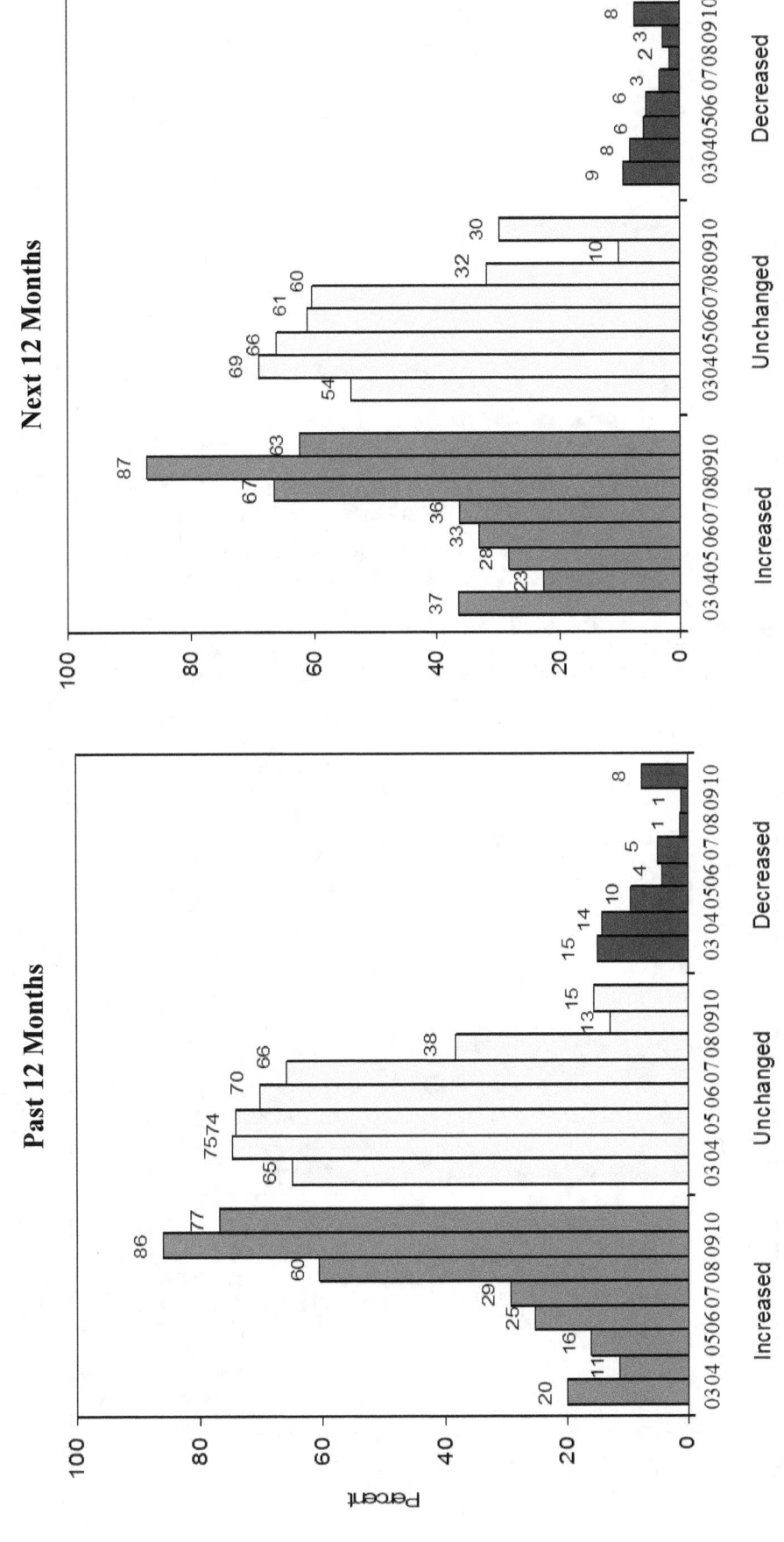

Figure 14: Retail Credit Risk Trends – Current Credit Risk Change, by Product Type

(Percent of Responses)

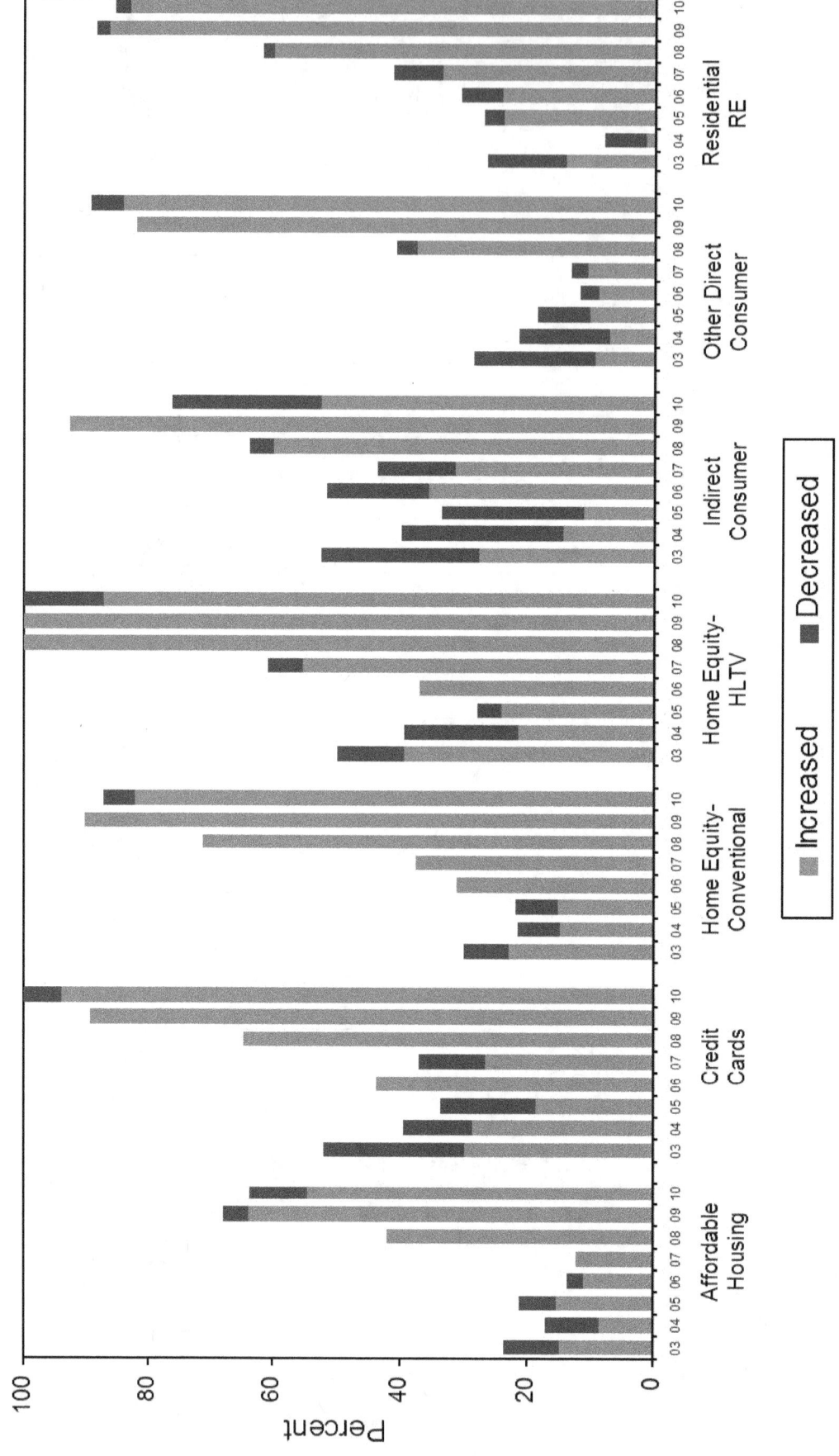

Part III: Data Tables

Note: Some percentages in tables and figures do not add to 100 because of rounding.

Commercial Lending Portfolios

Agricultural Lending

Thirteen of the 51 surveyed banks engaged in some form of agricultural lending.

Table 13: Changes in Underwriting Standards in Agricultural Loan Portfolios
(Percent of Responses)

	Eased	Unchanged	Tightened
2002	0	70	30
2003	0	67	33
2004	0	93	7
2005	0	93	7
2006	5	95	0
2007	10	80	10
2008	0	95	5
2009	0	75	25
2010	0	54	46

Table 14: Changes in the Level of Credit Risk in Agricultural Loan Portfolios
(Percent of Responses)

	Declined Significantly	Declined Somewhat	Unchanged	Increased Somewhat	Increased Significantly
2002	0	7	63	30	0
2003	0	11	48	41	0
2004	0	10	59	31	0
2005	4	17	69	10	0
2006	0	23	63	14	0
2007	0	0	55	45	0
2008	0	26	47	26	0
2009	0	6	38	56	0
2010	0	0	46	31	23
Future 12 Months	0	15	39	46	0

Asset-Based Loans

Thirteen surveyed banks engaged in asset-based lending.

Table 15: Changes in Underwriting Standards in Asset-Based Loan Portfolios
(Percent of Responses)

	Eased	Unchanged	Tightened
2002	3	66	31
2003	0	58	42
2004	16	71	13
2005	30	67	3
2006	30	57	13
2007	25	68	7
2008	9	70	22
2009	6	23	71
2010	8	31	61

Table 16: Changes in the Level of Credit Risk in Asset-Based Loan Portfolios
(Percent of Responses)

	Declined Significantly	Declined Somewhat	Unchanged	Increased Somewhat	Increased Significantly
2002	0	0	50	50	0
2003	3	26	42	29	0
2004	3	29	55	13	0
2005	0	24	52	24	0
2006	0	17	61	22	0
2007	0	14	43	43	0
2008	0	0	30	70	0
2009	0	0	12	70	18
2010	0	0	8	77	15
Future 12 Months	0	23	23	54	0

Commercial Leasing

Eleven of the surveyed banks engaged in commercial leasing.

Table 17: Changes in Underwriting Standards in Commercial Leasing Portfolios
(Percent of Responses)

	Eased	Unchanged	Tightened
2006	12	76	12
2007	26	69	5
2008	7	50	43
2009	0	40	60
2010	0	27	73

Table 18: Changes in the Level of Credit Risk in Commercial Leasing Portfolios
(Percent of Responses)

	Declined Significantly	Declined Somewhat	Unchanged	Increased Somewhat	Increased Significantly
2006	6	35	53	6	0
2007	0	16	63	21	0
2008	0	0	71	29	0
2009	0	0	13	80	7
2010	0	0	0	55	45
Future 12 Months	0	9	9	82	0

Commercial Real Estate Lending – Commercial Construction

Thirty-six of the surveyed banks engaged in commercial construction lending.

Table 19: Changes in Underwriting Standards in Commercial Construction Loan Portfolios
(Percent of Responses)

	Eased	Unchanged	Tightened
2003	2	61	37
2004	10	75	15
2005	29	63	8
2006	32	56	12
2007	28	59	13
2008	8	43	49
2009	0	20	80
2010	3	25	72

Table 20: Changes in the Level of Credit Risk in Commercial Construction Loan Portfolios
(Percent of Responses)

	Declined Significantly	Declined Somewhat	Unchanged	Increased Somewhat	Increased Significantly
2003	0	7	46	42	5
2004	0	7	59	34	0
2005	2	5	65	28	0
2006	0	5	65	30	0
2007	0	2	48	49	1
2008	0	0	22	69	8
2009	0	0	5	54	41
2010	0	5	3	50	42
Future 12 Months	0	8	17	64	11

Commercial Real Estate Lending – Residential Construction

Twenty-two of the surveyed banks engaged in residential construction lending.

Table 21: Changes in Underwriting Standards in Residential Construction Loan Portfolios
(Percent of Responses)

	Eased	Unchanged	Tightened
2003	0	76	24
2004	5	86	9
2005	21	72	7
2006	25	64	11
2007	17	50	33
2008	2	36	62
2009	0	8	92
2010	0	36	64

Table 22: Changes in the Level of Credit Risk in Residential Construction Loan Portfolios
(Percent of Responses)

	Declined Significantly	Declined Somewhat	Unchanged	Increased Somewhat	Increased Significantly
2003	0	2	62	34	2
2004	0	4	76	18	2
2005	2	6	65	27	0
2006	0	2	52	46	0
2007	0	4	27	63	6
2008	0	0	7	48	45
2009	0	0	0	34	66
2010	5	9	4	41	41
Future 12 Months	0	32	14	50	4

Commercial Real Estate Lending – Other

Forty-seven of the surveyed banks engaged in other commercial real estate lending.

Table 23: Changes in Underwriting Standards in Other Commercial Real Estate Loan Portfolios
(Percent of Responses)

	Eased	Unchanged	Tightened
2003	5	71	24
2004	8	83	9
2005	24	65	11
2006	32	60	8
2007	20	73	7
2008	2	73	25
2009	2	22	76
2010	2	38	60

Table 24: Changes in the Level of Credit Risk in Other Commercial Real Estate Loan Portfolios
(Percent of Responses)

	Declined Significantly	Declined Somewhat	Unchanged	Increased Somewhat	Increased Significantly
2003	0	5	48	43	4
2004	0	12	66	20	2
2005	2	9	65	24	0
2006	1	10	55	34	0
2007	0	2	59	38	1
2008	0	2	39	58	2
2009	0	2	5	67	26
2010	0	2	9	55	34
Future 12 Months	0	9	6	81	4

International Lending

Ten of the surveyed banks engaged in international lending.

Table 25: Changes in Underwriting Standards in International Loan Portfolios
(Percent of Responses)

	Eased	Unchanged	Tightened
2002	11	61	28
2003	6	55	39
2004	11	61	28
2005	27	73	0
2006	30	70	0
2007	30	70	0
2008	10	60	30
2009	0	13	87
2010	30	40	30

Table 26: Changes in the Level of Credit Risk in International Loan Portfolios
(Percent of Responses)

	Declined Significantly	Declined Somewhat	Unchanged	Increased Somewhat	Increased Significantly
2002	0	22	39	28	11
2003	0	6	55	33	6
2004	6	33	55	6	0
2005	0	20	73	7	0
2006	0	0	80	20	0
2007	0	0	70	30	0
2008	0	0	40	40	20
2009	0	0	0	63	37
2010	0	0	30	50	20
Future 12 Months	0	0	40	60	0

Middle Market Lending

Forty of the surveyed banks engaged in middle market lending.

Table 27: Changes in Underwriting Standards in Middle Market Loan Portfolios
(Percent of Responses)

	Eased	Unchanged	Tightened
2002	0	60	40
2003	6	63	31
2004	14	81	5
2005	28	67	5
2006	31	66	3
2007	33	60	7
2008	6	69	25
2009	0	33	67
2010	0	50	50

Table 28: Changes in the Level of Credit Risk in Middle Market Loan Portfolios
(Percent of Responses)

	Declined Significantly	Declined Somewhat	Unchanged	Increased Somewhat	Increased Significantly
2002	2	8	22	66	2
2003	0	13	39	44	4
2004	0	28	52	18	2
2005	4	26	54	16	0
2006	0	24	54	20	2
2007	0	5	51	44	0
2008	0	0	50	48	2
2009	0	2	6	88	4
2010	0	0	5	73	22
Future 12 Months	0	13	17	68	2

Small Business Lending

Thirty-two of the surveyed banks lent in the small business market.

Table 29: Changes in Underwriting Standards in Small Business Loan Portfolios
(Percent of Responses)

	Eased	Unchanged	Tightened
2002	2	66	32
2003	4	65	31
2004	11	74	15
2005	13	81	6
2006	19	76	5
2007	11	76	13
2008	11	72	17
2009	0	36	64
2010	0	34	66

Table 30: Changes in the Level of Credit Risk in Small Business Loan Portfolios
(Percent of Responses)

	Declined Significantly	Declined Somewhat	Unchanged	Increased Somewhat	Increased Significantly
2002	0	2	56	40	2
2003	0	4	56	38	2
2004	0	15	72	13	0
2005	0	11	70	19	0
2006	0	5	71	22	2
2007	2	4	66	26	2
2008	0	3	36	58	3
2009	0	2	14	72	12
2010	0	9	6	66	19
Future 12 Months	0	3	22	72	3

Leveraged Loans

Sixteen of the surveyed banks engaged in leveraged loans.

Table 31: Changes in Underwriting Standards in Leveraged Loan Portfolios
(Percent of Responses)

	Eased	Unchanged	Tightened
2002	0	44	56
2003	0	48	52
2004	15	85	0
2005	32	68	0
2006	61	31	8
2007	67	33	0
2008	20	20	60
2009	0	31	69
2010	0	25	75

Table 32: Changes in the Level of Credit Risk in Leveraged Loan Portfolios
(Percent of Responses)

	Declined Significantly	Declined Somewhat	Unchanged	Increased Somewhat	Increased Significantly
2002	0	7	26	52	15
2003	10	33	28	29	0
2004	15	40	40	5	0
2005	5	27	58	5	5
2006	0	8	15	69	8
2007	0	13	34	53	0
2008	0	0	27	53	20
2009	0	0	6	63	31
2010	0	6	6	63	25
Future 12 Months	0	19	6	69	6

Large Corporate Loans

Twenty-nine of the surveyed banks were active in the large corporate loan market.

Table 33: Changes in Underwriting Standards in Large Corporate Loan Portfolios
(Percent of Responses)

	Eased	Unchanged	Tightened
2002	0	45	55
2003	3	49	48
2004	17	66	17
2005	32	68	0
2006	49	51	0
2007	40	60	0
2008	6	62	32
2009	0	40	60
2010	3	38	59

Table 34: Changes in the Level of Credit Risk in Large Corporate Loan Portfolios
(Percent of Responses)

	Declined Significantly	Declined Somewhat	Unchanged	Increased Somewhat	Increased Significantly
2002	0	8	29	53	10
2003	5	27	33	30	5
2004	17	36	36	11	0
2005	5	27	49	19	0
2006	0	19	46	32	3
2007	0	8	57	35	0
2008	0	0	47	47	6
2009	0	0	12	77	11
2010	0	3	0	76	21
Future 12 Months	0	17	21	62	0

Hedge Funds (Direct Credit Exposure)

Five of the surveyed banks engaged in direct lending to hedge funds.

Table 35: Changes in Underwriting Standards in Hedge Funds (Direct Credit Exposure)
(Percent of Responses)

	Eased	Unchanged	Tightened
2007	17	66	17
2008	0	100	0
2009	0	17	83
2010	0	40	60

Table 36: Changes in the Level of Credit Risk in Hedge Funds (Direct Credit Exposure)
(Percent of Responses)

	Declined Significantly	Declined Somewhat	Unchanged	Increased Somewhat	Increased Significantly
2007	0	0	83	17	0
2008	0	0	83	17	0
2009	33	0	0	34	33
2010	20	40	40	0	0
Future 12 Months	0	0	60	40	0

Hedge Funds (Counterparty Credit Exposure)

Six of the surveyed banks had sizable counterparty credit exposures to hedge funds.

Table 37: Changes in Underwriting Standards in Hedge Funds
(Counterparty Credit Exposure)
(Percent of Responses)

	Eased	Unchanged	Tightened
2007	29	71	0
2008	0	29	71
2009	0	14	86
2010	33	50	17

Table 38: Changes in the Level of Credit Risk in Hedge Funds
(Counterparty Credit Exposure)
(Percent of Responses)

	Declined Significantly	Declined Somewhat	Unchanged	Increased Somewhat	Increased Significantly
2007	0	14	72	14	0
2008	0	14	29	43	14
2009	0	0	14	57	29
2010	17	50	33	0	0
Future 12 Months	0	17	33	50	0

Retail Lending Portfolios

Affordable Housing Lending

Table 39: Twenty-two of the surveyed banks engaged in affordable housing lending.

Changes in Underwriting Standards in Affordable Housing Loan Portfolios
(Percent of Responses)

	Eased	Unchanged	Tightened
2002	3	91	6
2003	3	88	9
2004	6	86	8
2005	15	76	9
2006	3	97	0
2007	6	88	6
2008	3	74	23
2009	0	60	40
2010	0	59	41

Table 40: Changes in the Level of Credit Risk in Affordable Housing Loan Portfolios
(Percent of Responses)

	Declined Significantly	Declined Somewhat	Unchanged	Increased Somewhat	Increased Significantly
2002	0	6	73	21	0
2003	0	9	76	15	0
2004	0	9	82	9	0
2005	0	6	79	15	0
2006	0	3	86	11	0
2007	0	0	88	12	0
2008	0	0	58	35	6
2009	0	4	32	52	12
2010	0	9	36	46	9
Future 12 Months	0	9	36	55	0

Credit Card Lending

Sixteen of the surveyed banks engaged in credit card lending.

Table 41: Changes in Underwriting Standards in Credit Card Loan Portfolios
(Percent of Responses)

	Eased	Unchanged	Tightened
2002	12	66	22
2003	19	62	19
2004	18	61	21
2005	7	74	19
2006	19	56	25
2007	16	79	5
2008	18	47	35
2009	0	32	68
2010	0	19	81

Table 42: Changes in the Level of Credit Risk in Credit Card Loan Portfolios
(Percent of Responses)

	Declined Significantly	Declined Somewhat	Unchanged	Increased Somewhat	Increased Significantly
2002	0	6	54	31	9
2003	0	22	48	30	0
2004	0	11	61	25	3
2005	0	15	67	18	0
2006	0	0	56	44	0
2007	0	11	63	26	0
2008	0	0	35	65	0
2009	0	0	10	53	37
2010	0	6	0	63	31
Future 12 Months	0	0	38	56	6

Other Direct Consumer Lending

Nineteen of the surveyed banks engaged in other direct consumer lending.

Table 43: Changes in Underwriting Standards in Other Direct Consumer Loan Portfolios
(Percent of Responses)

	Eased	Unchanged	Tightened
2002	2	67	31
2003	8	68	24
2004	3	86	11
2005	6	82	12
2006	3	91	6
2007	8	87	5
2008	6	72	22
2009	4	28	68
2010	0	68	32

Table 44: Changes in the Level of Credit Risk in Other Direct Consumer Loan Portfolios
(Percent of Responses)

	Declined Significantly	Declined Somewhat	Unchanged	Increased Somewhat	Increased Significantly
2002	2	6	67	25	0
2003	2	17	72	7	2
2004	2	13	78	7	0
2005	0	8	82	10	0
2006	0	3	88	9	0
2007	0	3	87	10	0
2008	0	3	59	38	0
2009	0	0	18	68	14
2010	0	5	11	74	10
Future 12 Months	0	5	37	53	5

Home Equity – Conventional Lending

Forty of the surveyed banks offered the conventional home equity lending product.

Table 45: Changes in Underwriting Standards in Home Equity – Conventional Loan Portfolios
(Percent of Responses)

	Eased	Unchanged	Tightened
2002	0	74	26
2003	18	63	19
2004	13	77	10
2005	27	62	11
2006	34	64	2
2007	19	65	16
2008	2	46	52
2009	0	22	78
2010	5	35	60

Table 46: Changes in the Level of Credit Risk in Home Equity – Conventional Loan Portfolios
(Percent of Responses)

	Declined Significantly	Declined Somewhat	Unchanged	Increased Somewhat	Increased Significantly
2002	0	7	71	22	0
2003	4	4	69	23	0
2004	0	6	79	13	2
2005	0	7	78	15	0
2006	0	0	69	29	2
2007	0	0	63	34	3
2008	0	0	29	52	19
2009	0	0	10	63	27
2010	0	5	12	73	10
Future 12 Months	0	10	25	65	0

Home Equity – High LTV Lending

Eight of the surveyed banks offered the high LTV home equity lending product.

Table 47: Changes in Underwriting Standards in Home Equity – High LTV Loan Portfolios
(Percent of Responses)

	Eased	Unchanged	Tightened
2002	0	56	44
2003	7	68	25
2004	18	71	11
2005	24	56	20
2006	37	63	0
2007	22	61	17
2008	6	6	89
2009	0	7	93
2010	0	13	87

Table 48: Changes in the Level of Credit Risk in Home Equity – High LTV Loan Portfolios
(Percent of Responses

	Declined Significantly	Declined Somewhat	Unchanged	Increased Somewhat	Increased Significantly
2002	0	12	40	44	4
2003	0	11	50	36	3
2004	0	18	61	18	3
2005	0	4	72	24	0
2006	0	0	63	37	0
2007	0	6	39	55	0
2008	0	0	0	56	44
2009	0	0	0	36	64
2010	0	13	0	50	37
Future 12 Months	0	13	12	63	12

Indirect Consumer Lending

Twenty-one of the surveyed banks engaged in indirect consumer lending.

Table 49: Changes in Underwriting Standards in Indirect Consumer Loan Portfolios
(Percent of Responses)

	Eased	Unchanged	Tightened
2002	0	72	28
2003	5	65	30
2004	11	60	29
2005	25	61	14
2006	35	52	13
2007	16	75	9
2008	20	56	24
2009	0	26	74
2010	5	33	62

Table 50: Changes in the Level of Credit Risk in Indirect Consumer Loan Portfolios
(Percent of Responses)

	Declined Significantly	Declined Somewhat	Unchanged	Increased Somewhat	Increased Significantly
2002	3	13	38	43	3
2003	5	20	47	28	0
2004	0	26	60	14	0
2005	3	19	67	8	3
2006	6	10	48	36	0
2007	0	3	87	10	0
2008	0	4	36	60	0
2009	0	0	7	74	19
2010	0	24	24	47	5
Future 12 Months	0	10	33	57	0

Residential Real Estate Lending

Forty-two of the surveyed banks engaged in residential real estate lending.

Table 51: Changes in Underwriting Standards in Residential Real Estate Loan Portfolios
(Percent of Responses)

	Eased	Unchanged	Tightened
2002	4	83	13
2003	2	86	12
2004	7	86	7
2005	22	73	5
2006	26	69	5
2007	19	67	14
2008	0	44	56
2009	0	27	73
2010	5	36	59

Table 52: Changes in the Level of Credit Risk in Residential Real Estate Loan Portfolios
(Percent of Responses)

	Declined Significantly	Declined Somewhat	Unchanged	Increased Somewhat	Increased Significantly
2002	0	8	68	24	0
2003	0	12	74	12	2
2004	0	6	92	2	0
2005	0	3	73	24	0
2006	0	7	69	24	0
2007	2	6	59	33	0
2008	2	0	38	55	5
2009	0	2	12	69	17
2010	0	3	14	57	26
Future 12 Months	0	7	26	67	0